HAL LEONARD GUITAR METHOD

PEDAL STEEL GUITAR

BY JOHNIE HELMS

To access audio visit:
www.halleonard.com/mylibrary

3216-2573-3709-3520

ISBN 0-634-08412-7

HAL•LEONARD®
7777 W. BLUEMOUND RD. P.O. BOX 13819 MILWAUKEE, WI 53213

In Australia Contact:
Hal Leonard Australia Pty. Ltd.
4 Lentara Court
Cheltenham, Victoria, 3192 Australia
Email: ausadmin@halleonard.com.au

Visit Hal Leonard Online at
www.halleonard.com

T0052403

ABOUT THE AUTHOR

Johnie Helms comes from a musical family and started on standard guitar at age twelve. During high school Johnie played bass guitar for several local bands, usually three nights a week, in area clubs.

Johnie has toured professionally for over fifteen years, playing both pedal steel and slide guitar for many famous country artists both old and new, his longest stint being with country superstar Toby Keith for ten years. He has also played on over 700 recording sessions to date and has an instrumental CD of his own.

Johnie has appeared on numerous television performances such as Austin City Limits, ABC Spring Break, the Academy of Country Music Awards, CBS Early Show, and the Country Music Awards. In 2002, he was nominated as instrumentalist of the year in the pedal steel guitar category by the Academy of Country Music.

ACKNOWLEDGMENTS

Thanks for the support and assistance of my family, Leonora Clancy, Steve Guilford, Ken Collins, Gibson/Epiphone, Peavey Electronics, Sound Tech-Washburn, Crate/Alvarez, and Eminence Speakers.

Johnie dedicates this book to his father, George Helms, and to Vernon Page, for sharing their love for and knowledge of the steel guitar, and for being his mentors and inspiration.

A BRIEF HISTORY

Descending originally from the Hawaiian lap steel, the pedal steel guitar has undergone many changes throughout its history. The early non-pedal 6-string models were very limited in the number of chords and intervals that could be played with only one tuning. When multi-neck non-pedal guitars were introduced, the player was allowed more chordal flexibility, simply by using different tunings on each neck; during the early 1940s these instruments could be heard on many country music recordings.

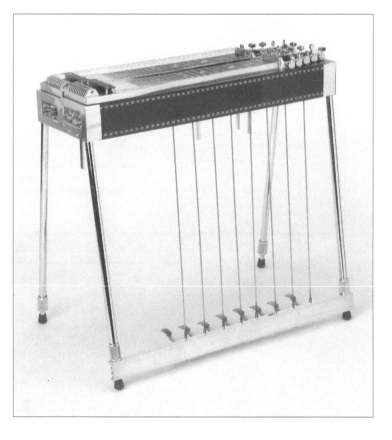

The pedal steel guitar as we know it today is a remarkable advancement in comparison to the crude designs of yesteryear, where you would find everything from coat hangers to cables pulling a single string through a simple hole drilled through the headstock and attached to a single pedal. Further improvements led to complex systems utilizing a series of steel cables and pulleys under the guitar, which in turn allowed the player multiple pedal options and better chordal flexibility on fewer necks.

Today's modern pedal steel guitars are constructed using lightweight materials and scientific designs incorporating the use of rods and levers, providing a more reliable, trouble-free instrument with complete flexibility.

INTRODUCTION AND SETUP

Starting with the basic construction of the pedal steel guitar, this book is for the novice who is unfamiliar with the instrument. Everything is written in easy-to-understand text and tablature, so it is not necessary to read music to use this book.

The course is designed for an E9 pedal steel guitar with three **pedals** (A, B, and C) and three **knee levers** (D, F, and E). The instrument pictured in this method is a double-neck pedal steel guitar. We will focus on the E9 neck only, which is the neck farthest away as you are sitting at the instrument. Notice that there are quite a few pedals and knee levers. You'll only need to use three pedals and three knee levers to play the E9 neck.

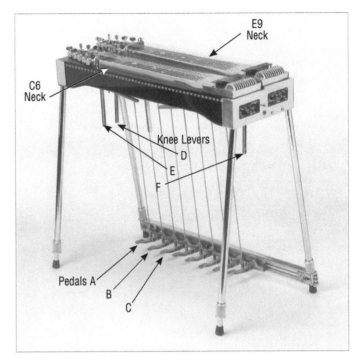

Pedals and Knee Levers

As you can see in Figure 1, there are a series of rods and shafts underneath the guitar.

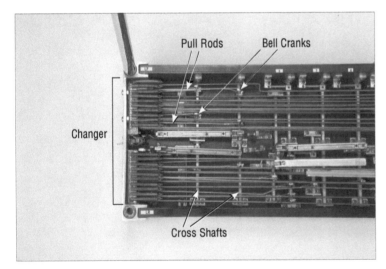

Figure 1: Underneath the Guitar

The **pull rods** are the smaller rods that run from left to right. They run from the **changer** to a series of what are called **bell cranks**. The bell cranks are attached to the larger shafts that run from the front of your guitar to its rear. These larger shafts are called **cross shafts**.

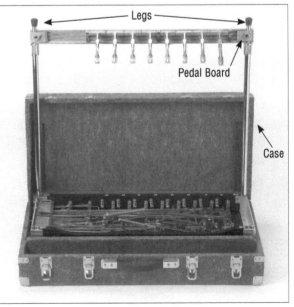

Figure 2: Guitar in Case

Start with the guitar in its open case, face down on the floor. Attach two **legs** onto the front of the guitar, then take your **pedal board** and attach it to these two front legs (Figure 2).

Look at one of your **pedal rods** and you'll notice a hook at one end and a coupling at the other end. Attach the hook end to the **pedal rod lever** located on the cross shaft towards the front of the guitar (Figure 3).

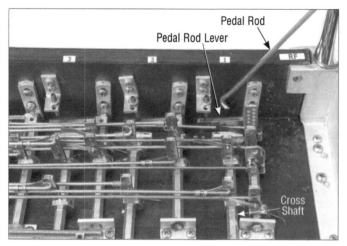

Figure 3: Attaching Pedal Rods A1

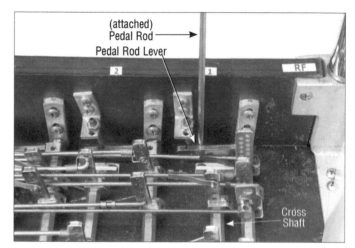

Figure 3: Attaching Pedal Rods A2

Now attach the coupling end of the pedal rod to the **pedal** (Figure 4).

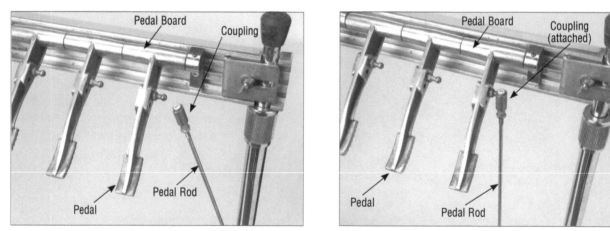

Figure 4: Attaching Pedal Rods B1

Figure 4: Attaching Pedal Rods B2

Repeat the procedure for the other pedals. When you have them all connected, attach the two rear legs.

Once you've completed this, you are ready to remove the guitar from its case. Place your right hand on the right front leg near the body of the guitar, and place your left hand on the left rear leg. Lift up and flip the guitar in an outward motion. The guitar should be facing you as you set it back down.

Sit behind your guitar and take a look at it for a moment. On your right-hand side you'll see the strings wrapping around a round bar (Figure 5). This is the top side of the changer that was mentioned earlier. The changer is actually a series of individual fingers referred to as **split fingers**. Directly in front of the changer and underneath the strings is the **pickup**; this "picks up" the vibrations of the strings which ultimately come through the amplifier.

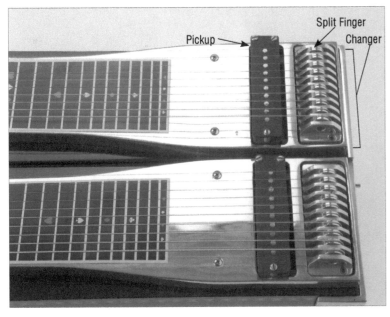

Figure 5: The Changer

At the rear of your guitar you'll see the nylon **tuners** (Figure 6). This is where you will tune your pedals and knee levers.

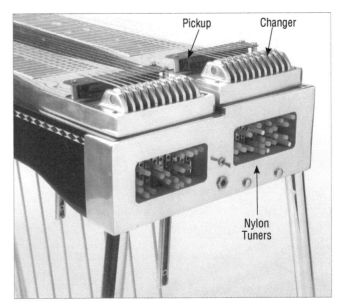

Figure 6: Nylon Tuners

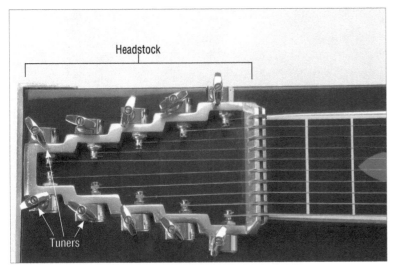

Figure 7: Headstock and Tuners

On the left-hand side you'll see the **headstock** (Figure 7), which is where you'll tune the strings of your guitar to their correct "open" pitches.

ACCESSORIES AND NECESSITIES

Pictured below are the items you'll need to properly tune, play, and amplify your pedal steel guitar.

Tuning Wrench

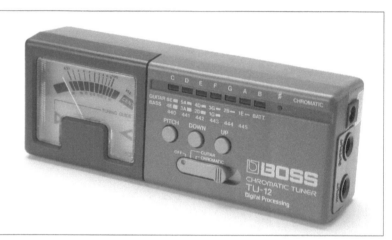

Chromatic Electronic Tuner

Steel Guitar Bar

Steel Guitar Seat

Steel Guitar Amplifier

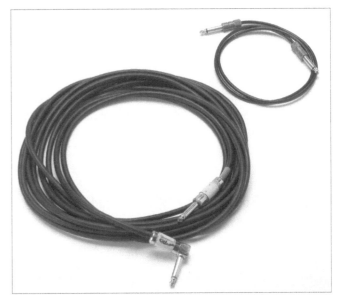

Cords for Amplifier and Volume Pedal

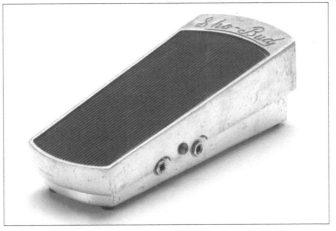

Volume Pedal

PICKS

Start by placing the thumb pick on your thumb, and one pick each on the index and middle fingers. Finger picks should be placed with the band of the pick across the fingernail and the tip bent back slightly towards your fingertip.

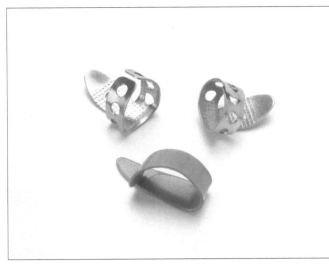

Finger Picks and Thumb Pick

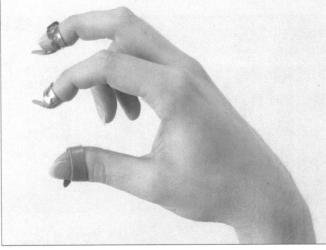

Wearing Picks

TUNING

Often learning to tune the pedal steel guitar can seem as challenging as learning to play. It is mandatory to use **tempered tuning** in order for the notes to blend with their respective chords. You can see this in the first column of the chart below, which shows the distances of the different notes from **concert pitch** (**A440**), in which the note A vibrates at exactly 440 cycles per second. Note that the number in the first column is not the actual pitch of each string—it shows the distance the note A would be tuned away from 440 if it were tuned the way each string needs to be tuned. In practical application, this means the first string, F#, is tuned approximately seven cents **sharp** (the actual pitch is around 743.05 cycles per second) when viewed on a standard electronic tuner. You can see that the next two strings should be tuned slightly below concert pitch, the fourth strings should be tuned slightly higher, and so on.

E9 TUNING CHART

Calibration (cycles/sec)	String	Gauge	Pitch	Pedals			Knee Levers		
				A	B	C	D	E	F
441.5	1	.013p	F#						
439	2	.015p	D#					D 439	
439	3	.011p	G#		A 441				
442.5	4	.014p	E			F# 439.5	D# 440		F 435.5
442	5	.017p	B	C# 438.5		C# 438.5			
439	6	.020p	G#		A 441				
441.5	7	.026w	F#						
442.5	8	.030w	E				D# 440		F 435.5
441.5	9	.034w	D					C# 438.5	
442	10	.038w	B	C# 438.5					

① F#
② D#
③ G#
④ E
⑤ B
⑥ G#
⑦ F#
⑧ E
⑨ D
⑩ B

You should buy an electronic tuner that has a **calibration** feature so that these tuning changes may be accomodated. Of course, it also critically important to learn to tune by ear.

If you loosen a string by turning its tuning key, its pitch will become lower; if you tighten the string, the pitch will become higher. When two pitches sound exactly the same, they are said to be **in tune** with each other.

If you accidentally tighten a string too much you may break it, but don't worry; it happens to everyone, and strings are inexpensive. The correct gauges of the strings that most players use are shown in the third column of the diagram. The first six strings are plain steel (p), and the last four are wound (w).

You'll also need to change your strings when they go "dead" in tone. This is caused by exposure to the air and the oils in your fingers, so keeping the guitar covered when you're not playing it, cleaning the strings, and washing your hands before playing will make the strings last longer.

OPEN STRINGS

The **open strings** of the guitar, or strings that aren't pedal- or level-shifted, should be tuned first. Start from the first string and work back to the tenth string. Track 1 plays these notes. If you don't have much experience tuning, you may need to pause the track and go through the tuning process more than once.

Instead of tuning a **sharp** string (too high in pitch) down to pitch, it's more effective to loosen it a little and then tune it up. Tuning up allows the string tension to remove the play between the tuning peg gears (as well as any other mechanical slack in the system), which will help the string stay in tune longer. So if you begin with a string that is sharp, tune it down first, and then bring it back up to pitch.

 Tuning Open Strings

TRACK 1

PEDALS AND LEVERS

When you have all the open strings tuned, hold down each pedal and lever in turn and pick the strings indicated to tune their correct pedal- or lever-shifted pitches as shown in the previous diagram. Use your tuning wrench on the nylon tuners on the back of the guitar for this.

 Tuning the A Pedal
Strings 5 and 10

TRACK 2

 Tuning the D Lever
Strings 4 and 8

TRACK 5

 Tuning the B Pedal
Strings 3 and 6

TRACK 3

 Tuning the F Lever
Strings 4 and 8

TRACK 6

 Tuning the C Pedal
Strings 4 and 5

TRACK 4

 Tuning the E lever
String 2

TRACK 7

9

RIGHT- AND LEFT-HAND TECHNIQUE

Start by placing the edge of your right hand on top of the strings, just to the left of the pickup. If you make a loose, relaxed fist, you'll notice your fingers are curved back toward you.

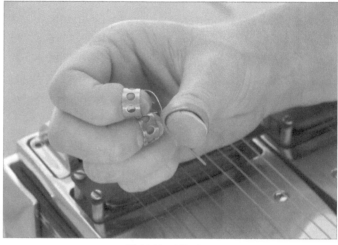

Right-Hand Posture

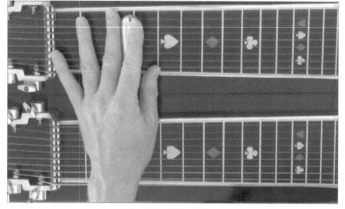

Right-Hand Position

Roll your right hand down towards the strings to the point where, as you look down towards your hand, you see the knuckles of the index and middle fingers. The edge of your palm should now be off the strings, but still fairly close to them.

This is a good starting position for your right hand. Not all steel guitar players have the same technique; it is important that you develop a technique that is comfortable for you.

Place your left thumb toward the rear of the bar and your index finger across the top of the bar, with the tip of your index finger just to the right of center. Your middle finger should be to the left of the bar. Spread your ring and little fingers apart behind the bar and let them touch the strings. This will stop unwanted overtones from being generated by the part of the string behind the bar.

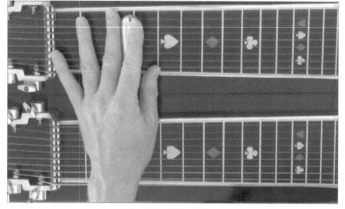

Left-Hand Position

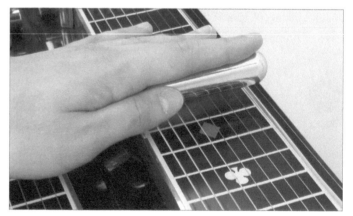

Holding the Bar

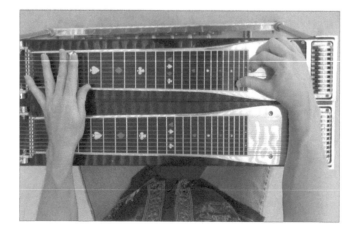

TABLATURE

In music diagrammed for pedal steel guitar, there are ten spaces, with each space representing a string.

In the diagram below are six figures that illustrate the tablature for most of the playing moves you'll encounter.

1. In Figure 1, the first column of the diagram, we see the spaces numbered 1 to 10 on the left side of the page, indicating the string numbers.

2. In Figure 2, the second column, the fret location where the bar is to be placed is indicated by a number located within a space. The fifth string is picked. Even though the pedal steel guitar is technically "fretless," we will often refer to the fret locations as frets or fret markers throughout the book.

3. In Figure 3 we see notes aligned vertically. They should be played together.

4. Figure 4 shows a line between notes. Sometimes an arched line is used. Both mean the bar is slid to another position and/or a pedal or knee lever is released or pushed, without picking the later notes on the right-hand side of the line. In this case, no pedals are used, and the bar is moved from the 3rd to the 5th fret.

5. In Figure 5 we see pedals and knee levers indicated next to the fret number. In this book, only the strings affected by the pedal changes have letters. In other books, the pedal and lever letters are sometimes written below the tablature. In either case, these pedals and/or levers should usually be depressed before you pick the strings.

6. Figure 6 tells us to play strings 8, 6, and 5 at the third fret with the A and B pedals down, then release pedals A and B. The lowest note is followed by a dotted line. This means to let this note continue to ring while the other notes are changing.

Figure 1	Figure 2	Figure 3	Figure 4	Figure 5	Figure 6
1					
2					
3					
4			3 —— 5		
5	3	5	3 —— 5	5a	3a —— 3
6		5	3 —— 5	5b	3b —— 3
7					
8		5		5	3 - - - - - -
9					
10					

MUSIC NOTATION

This book uses **standard notation** along with the pedal steel tablature, as described above. See the Appendix in the back of the book for the basics of standard notation. Though you can learn and play the music in this method with the tablature and audio alone, it is highly recommended that you learn to read music.

SCALES

A **scale** is a series of consecutive musical tones. An **interval** is the distance between any two tones. Scales are defined by the specific order of intervals between the notes.

MAJOR SCALE

A **major scale** contains five whole steps and two half steps, with the half steps between the 3rd and 4th, and between the 7th and 8th tones. The major scale represents the basic building blocks of Western music.

Play along with Track 8: the G major scale.

Track 9 is the G major scale an octave higher.

Many simple songs and licks are based entirely on one scale. Rather than write the correct sharps or flats needed to produce the scale every time they occur, a **key signature** is placed at the beginning of the notation. For instance, this example is in the key of G major, requiring every F to be raised to F#. Rather than write this sharp as an **accidental** every time there's an F in the music, the key signature for G major is used at the beginning (one sharp: F#).

A complete study of key signatures, key changes, and harmony is more than we should cover in a beginner's book. Right now, it's all about learning to play! So let's learn some hot licks!

LICKS

This book contains a total of twenty licks that every pedal steel player should know. You will find them throughout the book as you progress. These licks are used in song introductions and endings, in turnarounds (usually the last two measures of a repeated song form), as fills between lines or song sections, and in solos. These are all written and played in the key of G, but you should work them out in different keys and at various tempos until you can play them in any key without stopping to think.

LICK 1

TRACK 10

LICK 2

TRACK 11

LICK 3

TRACK 12

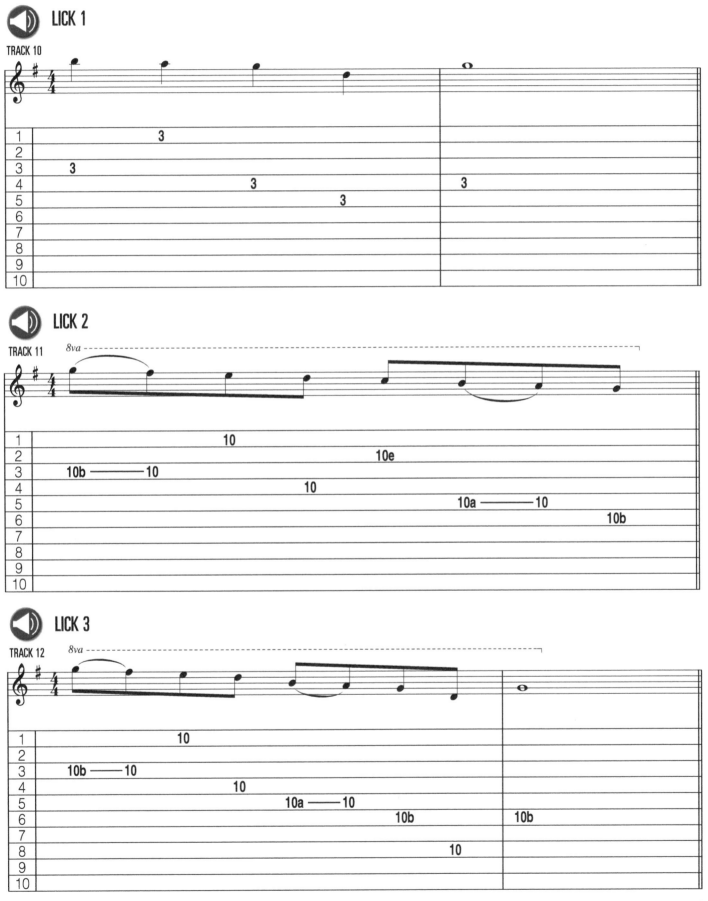

BASIC MAJOR CHORDS

Basic major chords, or **major triads**, consist of three notes: a root, 3rd, and 5th. These notes are the root, 3rd, and 5th degrees of the major scale. For example, if we build a major chord based on the notes of the C major scale: C D E F G A B C, then we'd have a chord with the notes C, E, and G.

We'll be covering strings 3, 4, 5, 6, 8, and 10. Any combination of three of these strings that provides the root, 3rd, and 5th can be used to create a major chord.

NO PEDALS

Strings 8, 6, and 5 are used in this example. If you play these three strings open (with no pedals, no levers, and no bar), you'll get an E chord, with the notes E, G#, and B.

Now, picking the same strings (8, 6, and 5), place your bar at the first fret for an F chord, third fret for a G chord, fifth fret for an A chord, seventh fret for a B chord, eighth fret for a C chord, tenth fret for a D chord, and twelfth fret for an E chord an octave higher than the first.

If you are a standard guitar player adding the pedal steel to your arsenal, you can roughly relate the notes of this chord shape to those found on the fourth, third, and second strings of an E-form barre chord.

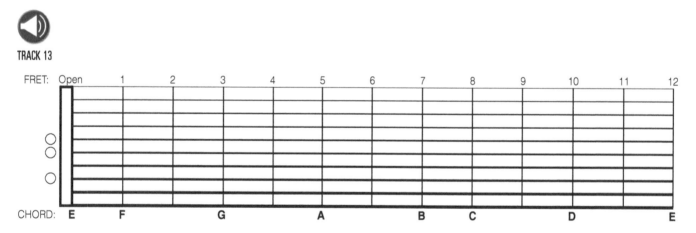

TRACK 13

You'll notice that some of the chords are one fret apart, while others are two frets apart, leaving some positions without their own unique letter name. These "in between" chords may be named with either sharps (#) or flats (♭) that refer to the chord immediately below or above. For instance, the chord at the 2nd fret, in between F and G, may be called F# or G♭.

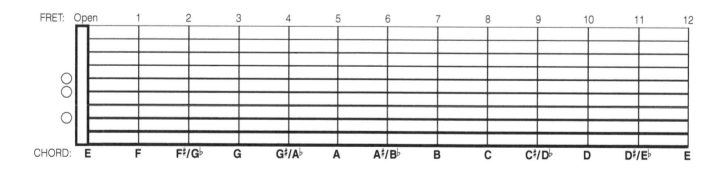

A AND B PEDALS

Now pick strings 6, 5, and 4 while depressing your A and B pedals, once again with no bar on the guitar. You'll get an open A chord, with the notes A, C♯, and E. Put your bar down at the second fret and pick the same strings for a B chord, then place the bar at the third fret for a C chord, fifth fret for a D chord, seventh fret for an E chord, eighth fret for an F chord, tenth fret for a G chord, and twelfth fret for an A chord an octave higher than the first.

This chord-producing combination of strings can be related to the top three strings of A-form barre chords on the standard guitar.

TRACK 14

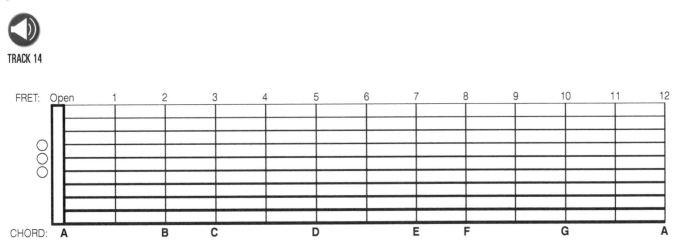

A PEDAL AND F LEVER

For another major chord pattern, raise your E strings with the F knee lever and depress the A pedal, and again pick strings 6, 5, and 4. Place your bar at the first fret for a D chord, third fret for an E chord, fourth fret for an F chord, sixth fret for a G chord, eighth fret for an A chord, tenth fret for a B chord, and eleventh fret for a C chord.

TRACK 15

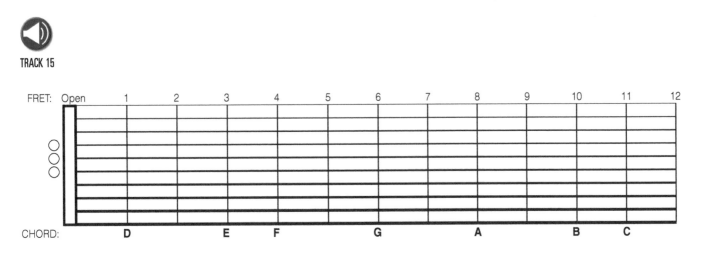

We can relate the notes of this chord shape to the top three strings of an open D major chord shape on a standard guitar, although on our open strings it starts a half step lower, on C♯ major, with the notes G♯, C♯, and E♯: the 5th, root, and 3rd.

LICKS

Try out the following licks that include major chords and the major scale.

 LICK 4

TRACK 16

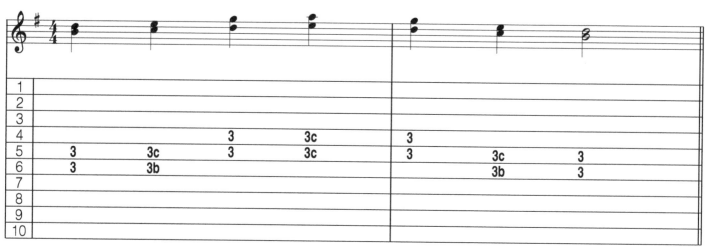

1								
2								
3								
4				3	3c	3		
5	3	3c	3	3c	3	3c	3
6	3	3b				3b	3
7								
8								
9								
10								

 LICK 5

TRACK 17

8va --

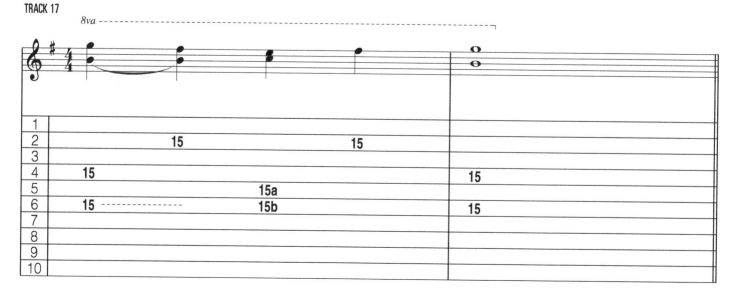

1				
2		15	15	
3				
4	15			15
5		15a		
6	15 -------------	15b		15
7				
8				
9				
10				

LICK 6

TRACK 18

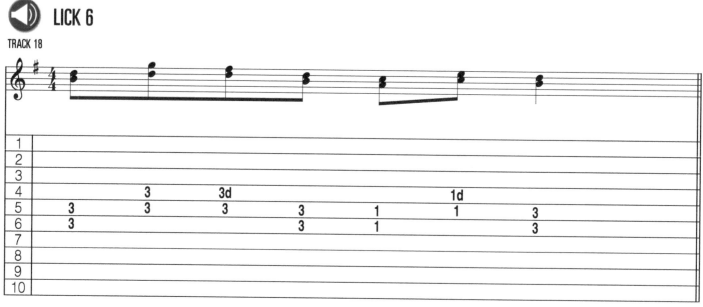

1								
2								
3								
4			3	3d		1d		
5	3	3	3	3	1	1	3
6	3			3	1		3
7								
8								
9								
10								

LICK 7

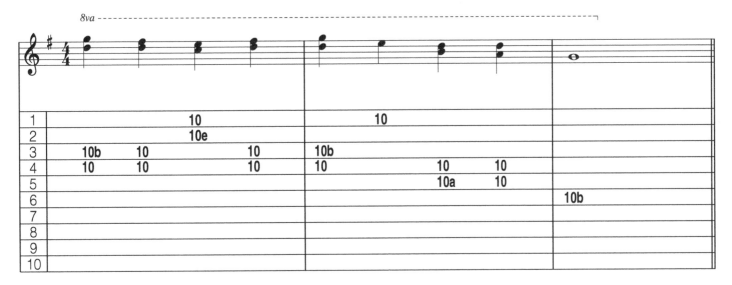

LICK 8

LEFT-HAND TIPS

- Keep the bar directly over the actual fret you are intending to play.
- Use only enough pressure downward on the bar to stop the strings from buzzing.

PICKUP NOTES

Music doesn't always begin on beat one. When you begin after beat one, the notes before the first full measure are called **pickup notes**.

COUNT: 4   &   1   2   3   4

Following is a lick that begins with a pickup note on beat four. Count the missing beats out loud before you begin playing.

 **LICK 9**

TRACK 21

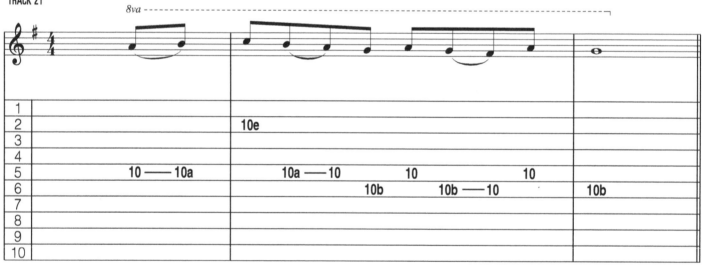

PRACTICE TIP

Regular practice is essential. Practicing a half hour each day is better than practicing two hours every four days. Find a regular time of the day that works for you.

GRACE NOTES

Many pedal steel licks make extensive use of **grace notes**. Usually they're played by picking a note and then immediately depressing a pedal or lever to get the "real" note, producing that distinctive bending sound. In tablature, grace notes look like any other note, but on the staff they are smaller and have a slash through them to signify that theoretically they don't take up any time in the music notation.

LICK 10
TRACK 22

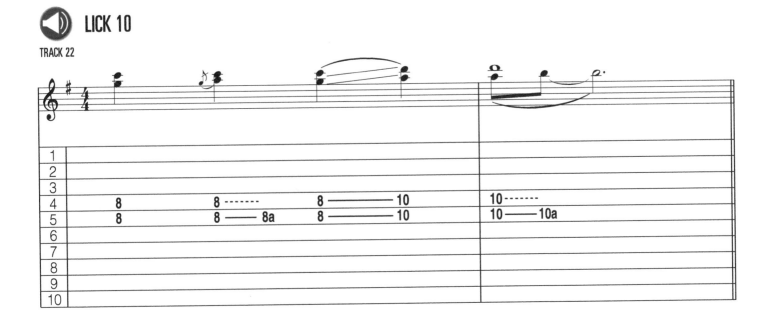

LICK 11
TRACK 23

SONGS

Throughout the book are some short tunes you can use to develop your playing. These should also be practiced in different keys, to help you learn to back singers with high or low vocal ranges.

TRACK 24
with steel guitar

TRACK 25
rhythm track

OLD TIME RELIGION

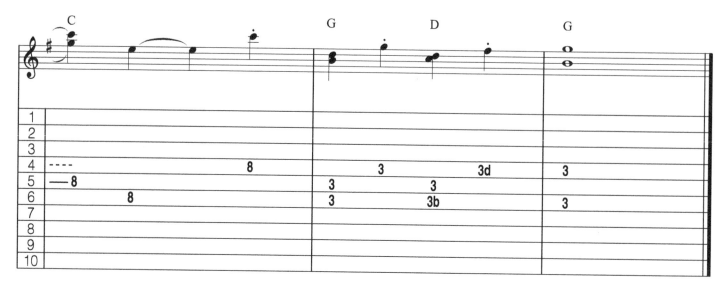

TRACK 26
with steel guitar

TRACK 27
rhythm track

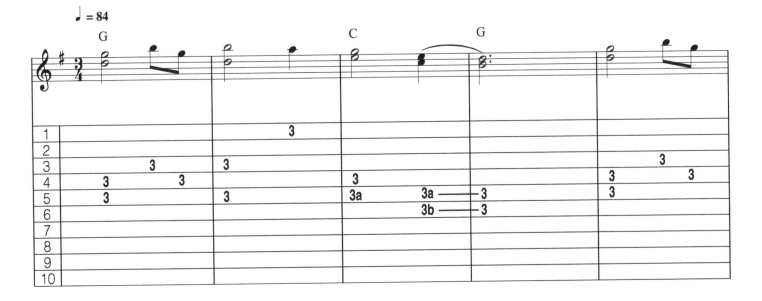

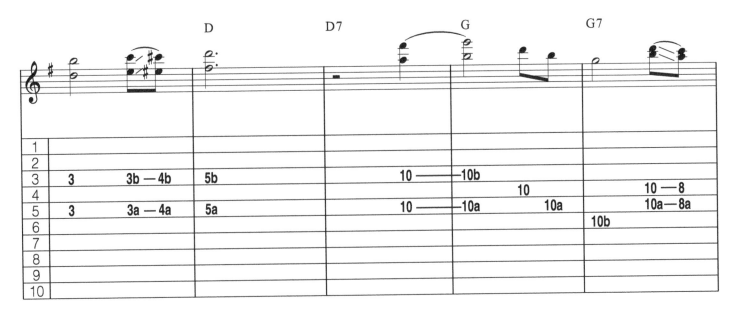

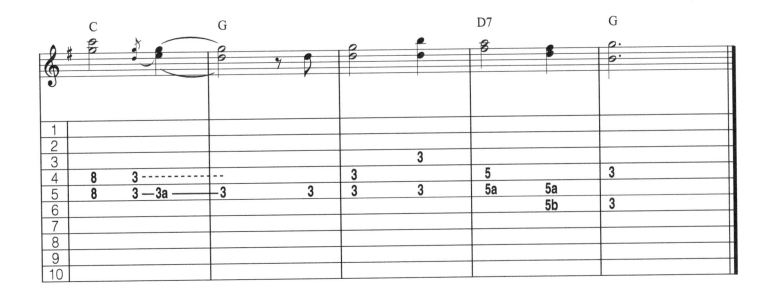

KEY POSITIONS

Here's how you can quickly find the standard chords commonly found within a song and its respective key.

I, IV, V

The most basic chords in any key are referred to as the **I**, **IV**, and **V**. They're based on the first, fourth, and fifth notes of the major scale.

Use the string combination of 6, 5, and 4 for all the chords. We'll use the key of G for this example. First we have G major, which is the I ("one") chord. Place your bar at the third fret and play a G chord with no pedals. If you depress your A and B pedals, you have C major, the IV chord. If you move up to the fifth fret with the A and B pedals still down, you'll have D major, the V chord in the key of G.

The V chord is often played as a dominant seventh chord, symbolized as **V7**. You can play D7 by moving the bar back to the third fret, depressing the B pedal and lowering the E notes on the guitar with the D knee lever. Another way to play D7 would be to go to the first fret and raise the E strings with the F knee lever. Finally, return to the third fret with no pedals to finish a simple progression with the G (I) chord.

TRACK 28

	I G	IV C	V D	V7 D7	V7 D7	I G
1						
2						
3						
4	3	3	5	3d	1f	3
5	3	3a	5a	3	1	3
6	3	3b	5b	3b	1	3
7						
8						
9						
10						

 **LICK 12**

TRACK 29

1				
2				
3				
4			3	3
5	3	3 —3a		
6	3	3 —3b		3
7				
8				
9				
10				

LICK 13

TRACK 30

 **LICK 14**

TRACK 31

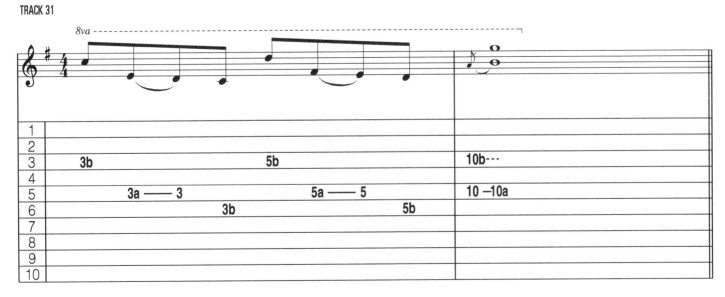

 **LICK 15**

TRACK 32

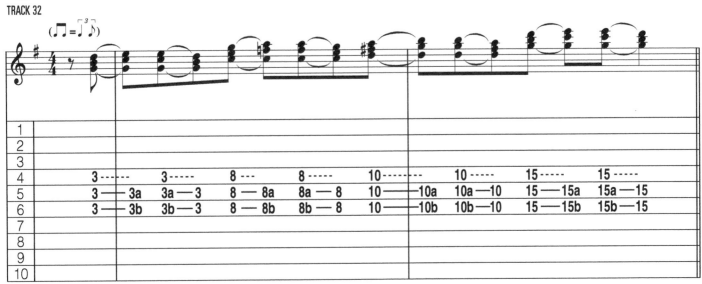

TRACK 33
with steel guitar

TRACK 34
rhythm track

THREE-STRING BOOGIE

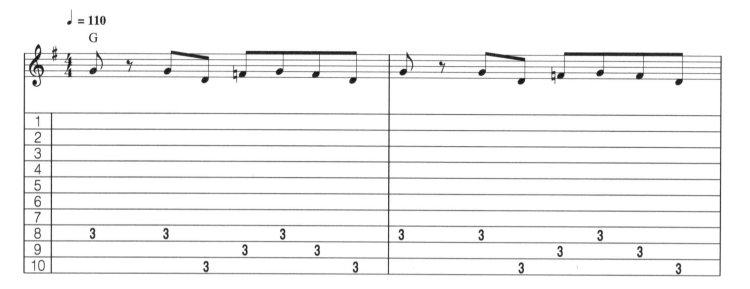

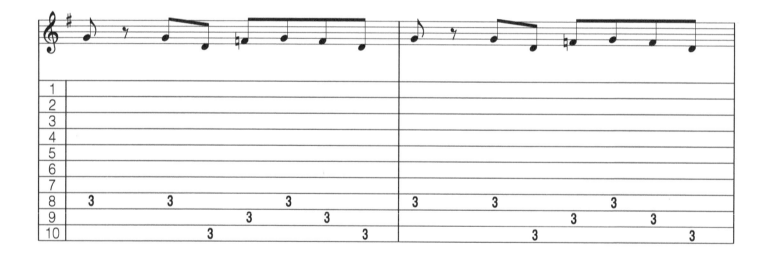

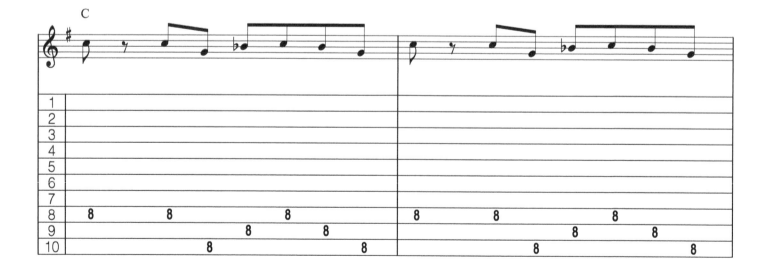

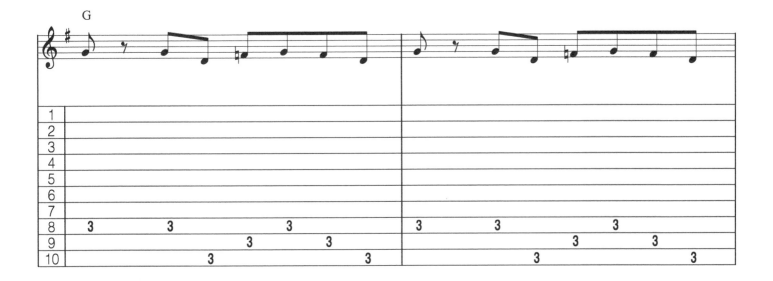

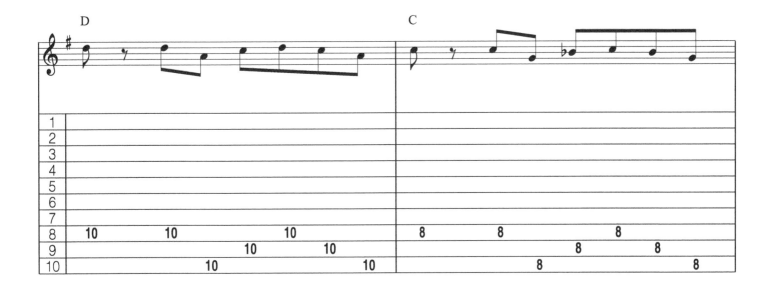

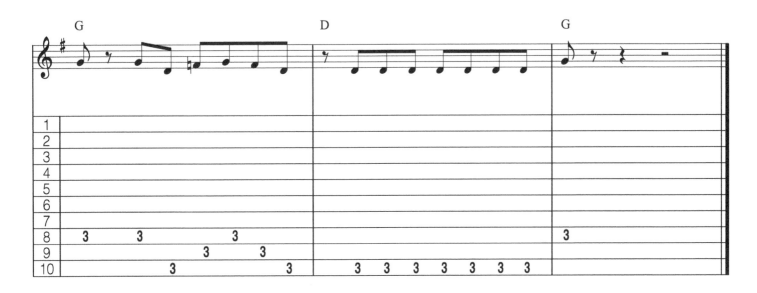

BASIC MINOR CHORDS

Like the major triad, the **minor triad** consists of a root, 3rd, and 5th. The difference is that its 3rd is lowered by one half step. The first major triad we spelled, C major, contained the notes C, E, and G. By lowering the 3rd (E) to E♭, we get a C minor triad: C–E♭–G.

A PEDAL

The open strings 8, 6, and 5 with the A pedal depressed give us a C♯ minor chord. Move the bar up to the fret numbers indicated in the diagram to obtain more minor chords. Placing the bar at the first fret gives us a D minor chord, which is where Track 35 starts.

TRACK 35

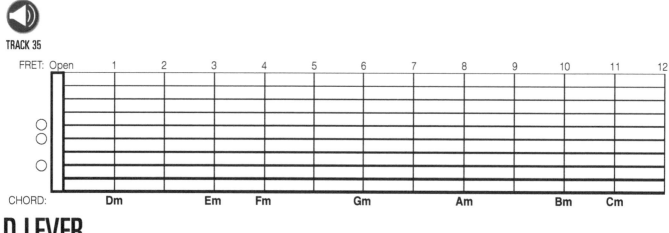

D LEVER

The open strings 6, 5, and 4 with the D knee lever depressed give us a G♯ minor chord. Move the bar up to the fret numbers indicated in the diagram to obtain more minor chords. Track 36 starts at the first fret with an A minor chord.

TRACK 36

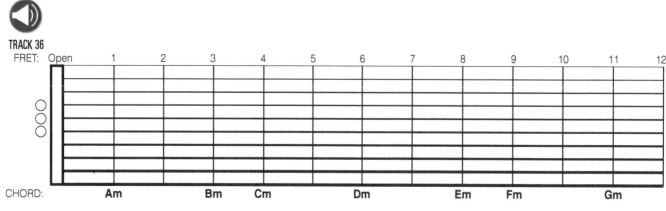

B AND C PEDALS

The open strings 5, 4, and 3 with the B and C pedals depressed give us an F♯ minor chord. Move the bar up to the fret numbers indicated in the diagram to obtain more minor chords. Track 37 starts at the first fret with a G minor chord.

TRACK 37

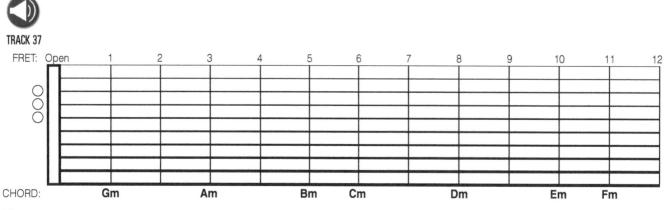

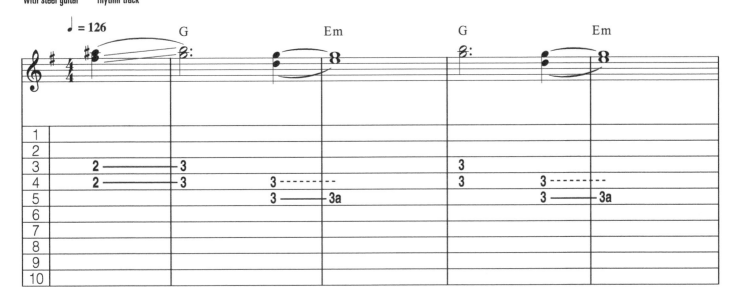

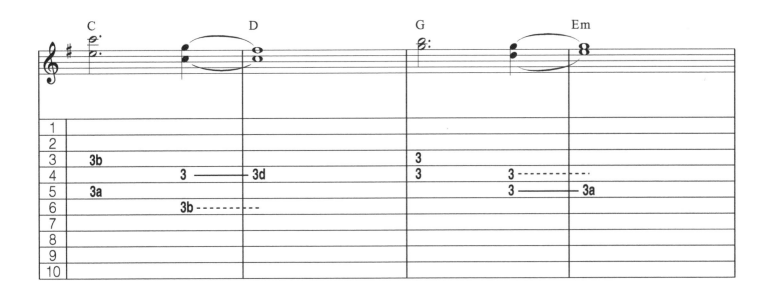

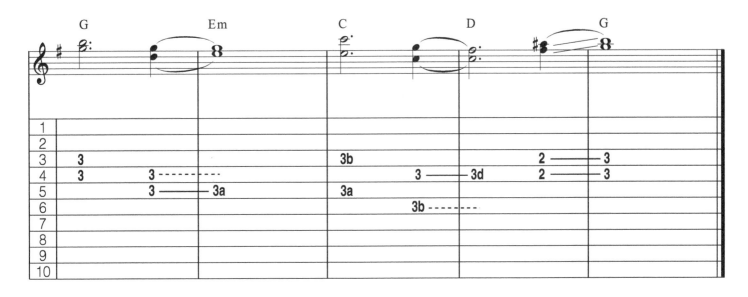

MINOR SCALES

HARMONIC MINOR SCALE

A **harmonic minor scale** may be formed by lowering the 3rd and 6th tones, resulting in half steps between the 2nd and 3rd tones, and between the 5th and 6th tones.

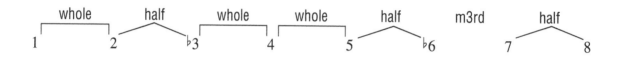

Play along with these two positions of the G harmonic minor scale.

TRACK 40

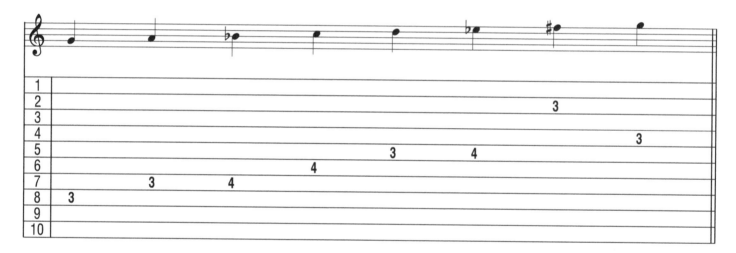

TRACK 41

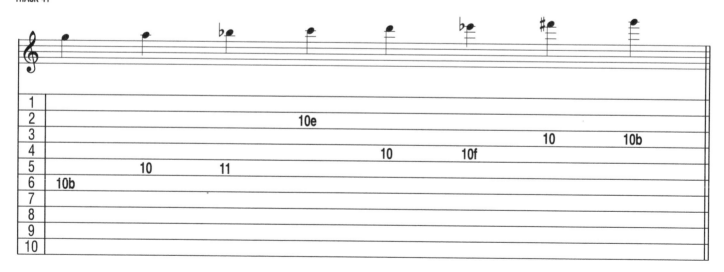

28

NATURAL MINOR SCALE

The **natural minor scale**, also known as a **relative minor scale**, is obtained when any major scale is played starting from its 6th degree. For example, if we count six scale steps up from G, we find E. The E natural minor scale is the relative minor of G major.

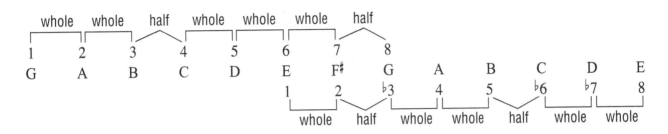

Play these two positions of the E natural minor scale.

TRACK 42

TRACK 43

GREENSLEEVES

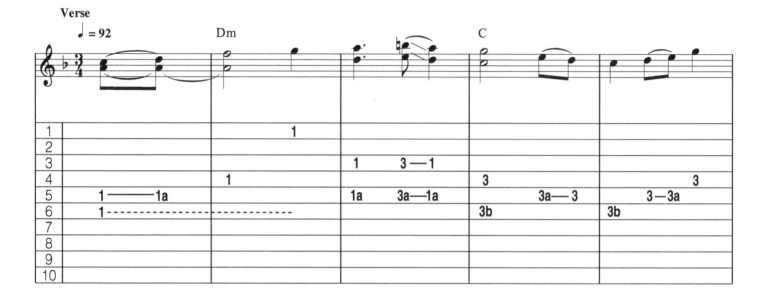

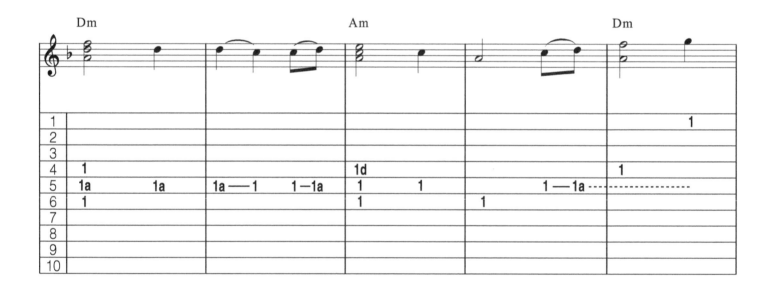

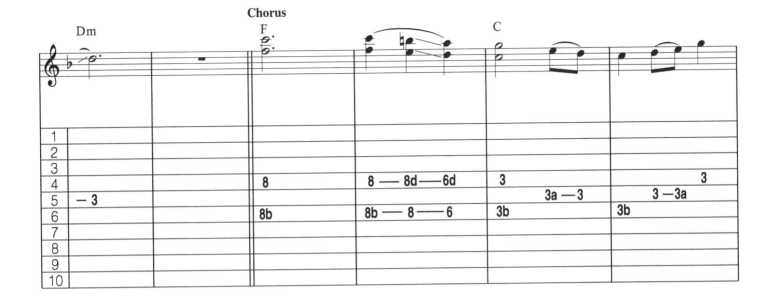

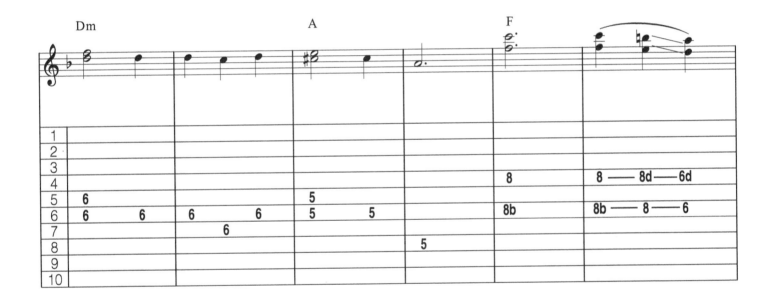

MORE KEY POSITIONS

vi, ii, iii

The next most important chord to learn is the **vi** minor chord. In the key of G this chord is E minor. With your bar at the third fret, depress the A pedal to get E minor.

To play the **ii** minor chord (Am), place your bar at the first fret and lower your E strings with the D knee lever. For the **iii** minor chord in G (Bm), move back up to the third fret, keeping your E strings lowered with the D knee lever.

All standard chord changes in any major key may be found within one whole step (two frets) below or above the third position I chord by using the patterns described below.

TRACK 46

	vi Em	ii Am	iii Bm
1			
2			
3			
4	3	1d	3d
5	3a	1	3
6	3	1	3
7			
8			
9			
10			

For your reference, here are the I, ii, iii, IV, V, and vi chords in several common keys.

Key (I)	ii	iii	IV	V	vi
C	Dm	Em	F	G	Am
D	Em	F#m	G	A	Bm
E	F#m	G#m	A	B	C#m
F	Gm	Am	B#	C	Dm
G	Am	Bm	C	D	Em
A	Bm	C#m	D	E	F#m
B	C#m	D#m	E	F#	G#m

OTHER CONCEPTS

THE SHUFFLE

In traditional music styles like country, blues, and jazz, eighth notes are played unevenly. This style of playing is known as **the shuffle** or swing feel.

You may have already heard the shuffle being played on some of the other recorded licks and songs.

Following is a graphic representation of the shuffle:

Play the first note twice as long as the second note.

Playing the eighth notes in this way will give you the desired shuffle or swing feel.

ARPEGGIO

An **arpeggio** is a "broken" chord whose notes are played individually and in succession instead of all at the same time. Arpeggios show up often in pedal steel guitar music.

CHORD

ARPEGGIO

RIGHT-HAND TIPS

- Pick strings close to the pickup, resting your hand just ahead of the bridge.

- As a general rule, most steel players use a plastic thumb pick, but some decide to use a metal thumb pick. The choice is up to the player.

BLOCKING

Blocking is when the vibrations of strings are **damped** to stop them from making unwanted sounds. The two types of blocking covered here are **pick blocking** and **palm blocking**. They are all that most players ever use.

Pick blocking is where you pick the string, then set a pick back down on the string in order to silence its vibration.

TRACK 47

Palm blocking involves using the edge of your right hand to damp the string. Lift your hand up slightly while you play the note, then place the edge of your hand back down to damp that note.

TRACK 48

The main difference between the two methods is that pick blocking is primarily used in fast to very fast situations (such as banjo roll-type picking), and palm blocking is used in slow to fast playing. I would suggest working on your palm blocking first, then as you become comfortable with it, move on to pick blocking.

A good blocking exercise is demonstrated on Track 49.

TRACK 49

With no bar on the guitar, pick string 1 with your index finger, then pick string 2 with your thumb. Next pick string 3 with your index finger, then pick string 4 with your thumb. Alternate between the finger and thumb all the way back to string 10, and then work your way back from string 10 to string 1. Apply palm blocking after each note.

When you have completed the exercise once, go back and play it again using the middle finger in place of the index finger.

			String	Finger		String	Finger
Index	=	I	1	I		1	M
Middle	=	M	2	T		2	T
Thumb	=	T	3	I		3	M
			4	T		4	T
			5	I		5	M
			6	T		6	T
			7	I		7	M
			8	T		8	T
			9	I		9	M
			10	T		10	T

Blocking is one of the more difficult things to master and does take a great deal of practice and patience, so start out slowly. Learn to keep a clean blocking technique so your playing doesn't sound sloppy and unclear.

STACCATO

One result of string blocking is the playing of notes in a separated, distinct manner known as **staccato**. When a note is to be played staccato, a dot is shown in the music directly above the notehead:

Following are some licks using staccato.

 LICK 16

TRACK 50

1				
2				
3				
4				
5	3 — 3a 8	10 –10a 10 –10a 8a —— 8	8 —— 3a —— 3	
6	3 — 3b 8	10 –10b 10 –10b 8b —— 8	8 —— 3b —— 3	
7				
8	3---- 8	10 --- 10 ---- 8 ---------	8 —— 3 ----------	
9				
10				

 LICK 17

TRACK 51

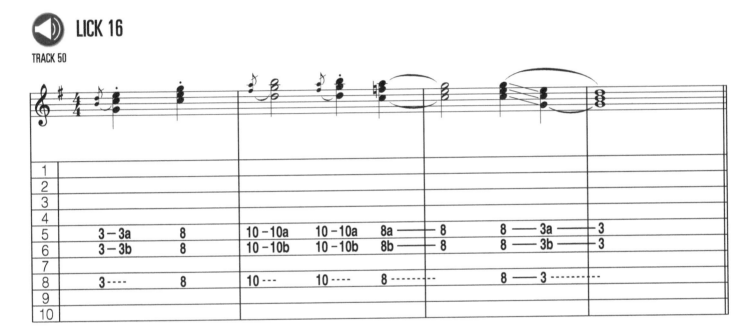

1				
2				
3				
4		10 --- 10 ---	10 10 --- 10 ----	
5	10	10 –10a 10a –10	10 10 –10a 10a –10	
6	10 –10b	10b		10b
7				
8	10			
9				
10				

MIDNIGHT SPECIAL

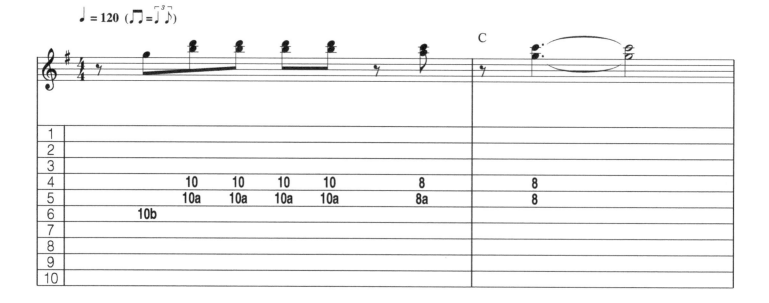

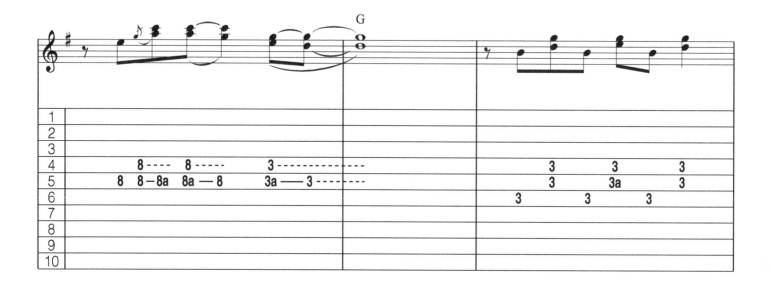

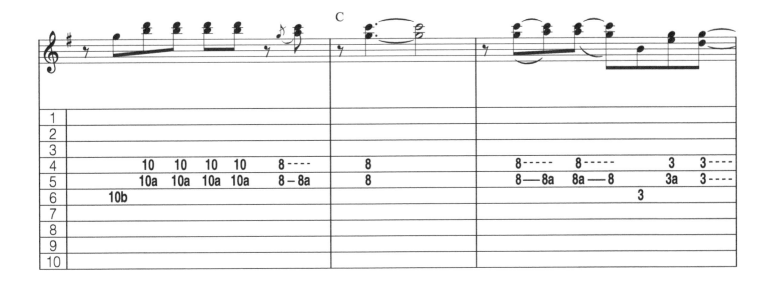

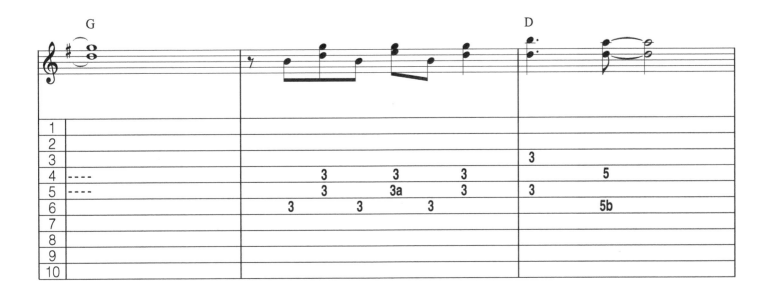

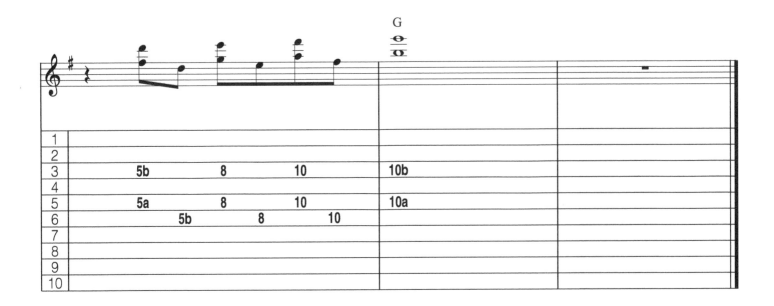

VIBRATO

Vibrato is the slight fluctuation of the pitch of a note. You will need to develop slow, medium, and fast vibrato. The decision about which is appropriate at a given time depends on the song. Vibrato is especially necessary for helping the pedal steel guitar sound in tune because it has no frets—only fret markers.

Start by placing your bar at the 3rd fret. Play strings 4 and 8, and then roll the bar back and forth slightly. Some people sweep the bar in a mild circular motion, but most use the rolling method.

TRACK 54

A faster vibrato would be used in a more rock 'n' roll type song to emulate slide guitar stylings.

TRACK 55

When we read tablature and notation, vibrato will be depicted with a squiggly line: ～～～～

 LICK 18

TRACK 56

1										
2										
3										
4		8	9	9—10	8 —— 6f	5	3 —— 3d	3	
5	10a	8a	9a	9a–10a	8a —— 6a	5a	3a —— 3	3	
6	10b								
7										
8										
9										
10										

VIBRATO TIP

- Move the bar back and forth with a rocking motion.
- Move the bar only $\frac{1}{8}$-inch away from and back to the fret.

BASIC DOMINANT 7TH CHORDS

This important chord type has a root, 3rd, 5th, and ♭7th.

F LEVER

With the F knee lever depressed, play strings 8, 6, and 5. This is a partial C#7 chord, without the root (C#). Now place your bar at the first fret and play along with Track 57, starting with a D7 chord.

TRACK 57

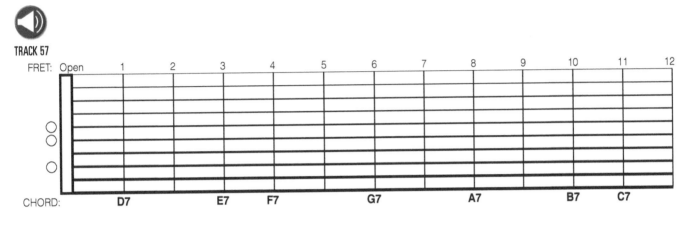

B PEDAL AND D LEVER

With the B pedal and D knee lever depressed, play strings 6, 5, and 4. This is a partial B7 chord, without the 5th (F#). Adding string 1 or 7 would include the 5th and complete the chord, though it's not really necessary. Now place your bar on the strings and play along with Track 58, starting with a C7 chord at the first fret.

TRACK 58

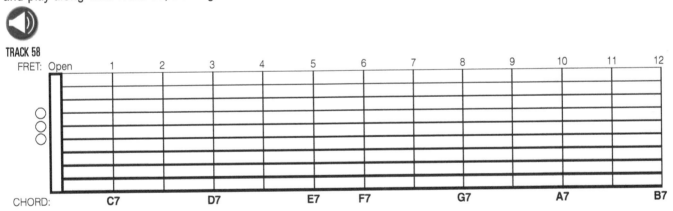

E LEVER

With the E knee lever depressed, play strings 5, 3, and 2. This is a partial E7 chord, without the root (E). Play along with Track 59, starting with an F7 chord at the first fret. The E lever lowers the second string one half step, giving the open dominant seventh chord sound. The ninth string may be added if your E lever has no effect on the second string.

TRACK 59

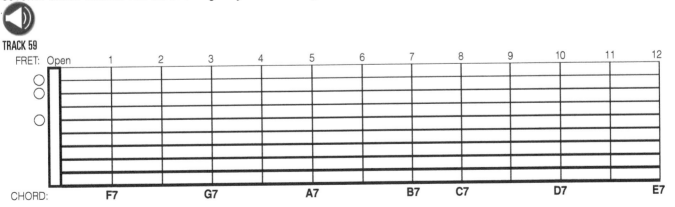

All the open strings of the E9 neck, with the exception of the second string, create an E dominant ninth chord (hence the instrument's name), so if you accidentally hit the wrong string, as long as you have the E lever depressed and the bar at the proper fret, you'll be adding another chord tone or an acceptable extension of a dominant seventh chord.

RED RIVER VALLEY

TRACK 60
with steel guitar

TRACK 61
rhythm track

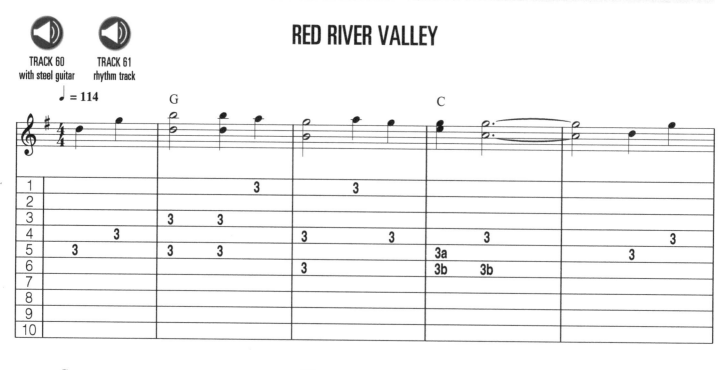

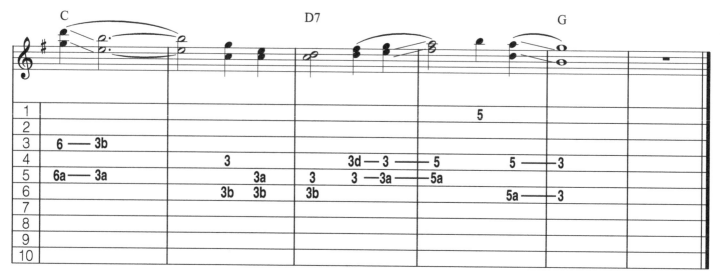

AURA LEE

TRACK 62
with steel guitar

TRACK 63
rhythm track

♩ = 80

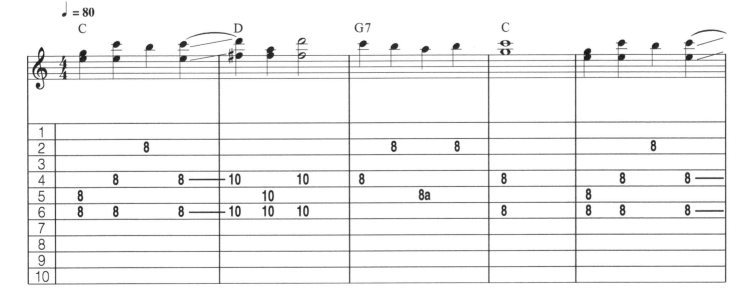

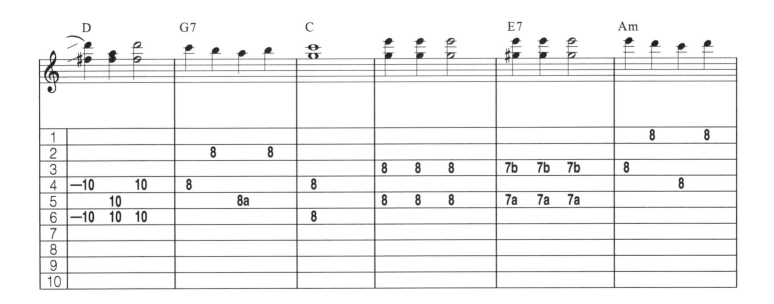

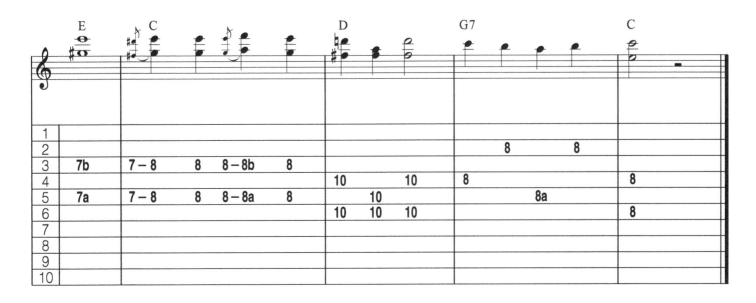

DOMINANT SCALE

MIXOLYDIAN MODE

A **dominant seventh scale**, also known as the **Mixolydian mode**, may be formed by lowering the 7th tone of the major scale by one half step.

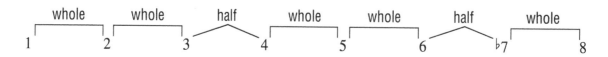

Here are two patterns of dominant scales in D to get you started on this important scale. These would fit over a D7, D9, or D13 chord.

TRACK 64

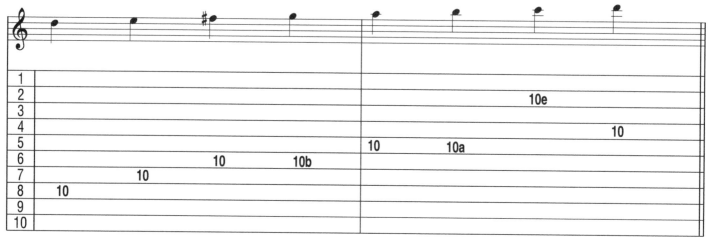

TRACK 65

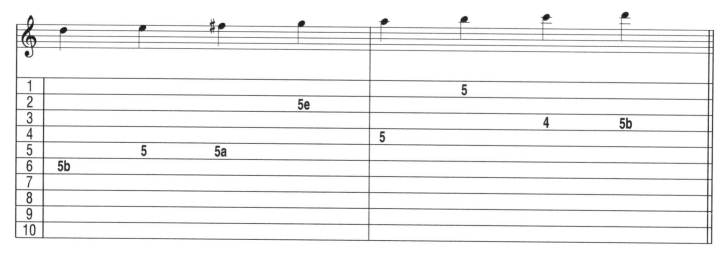

42

ROCKIN' PEDALS

♩ = 116

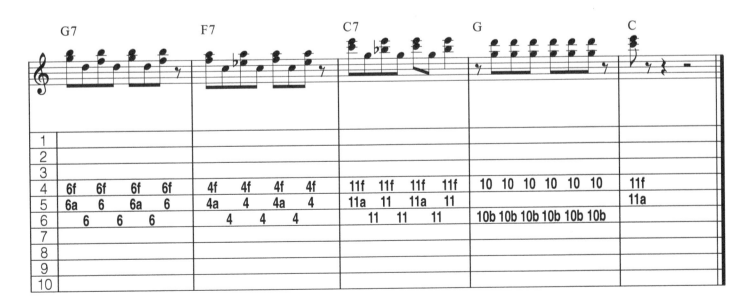

LICK 19

TRACK 68

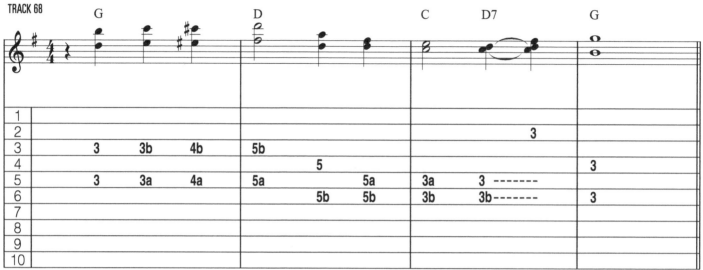

1									
2								3	
3	3	3b	4b	5b					
4					5				3
5	3	3a	4a	5a		5a	3a	3 -------	
6					5b	5b	3b	3b-------	3
7									
8									
9									
10									

 LICK 20

TRACK 69

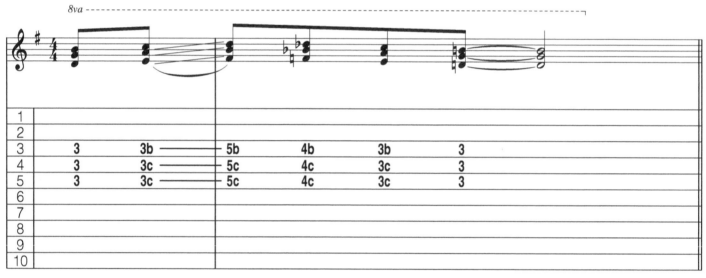

1						
2						
3	3	3b ———	5b	4b	3b	3
4	3	3c ———	5c	4c	3c	3
5	3	3c ———	5c	4c	3c	3
6						
7						
8						
9						
10						

TRACK 70   TRACK 71
with steel guitar   rhythm track

WHADA' SA

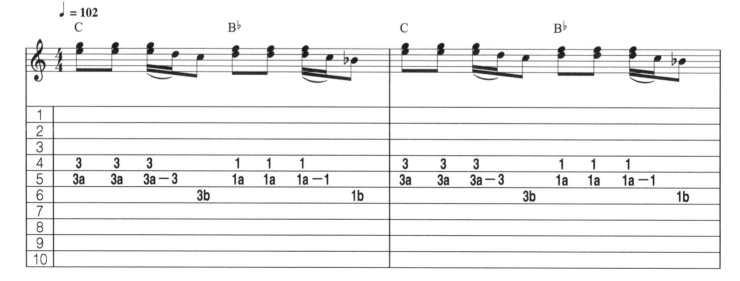

1												
2												
3												
4	3	3	3		1	1	1	3	3	3		1	1	1
5	3a	3a	3a—3		1a	1a	1a—1	3a	3a	3a—3		1a	1a	1a—1
6			3b				1b			3b				1b
7												
8												
9												
10												

44

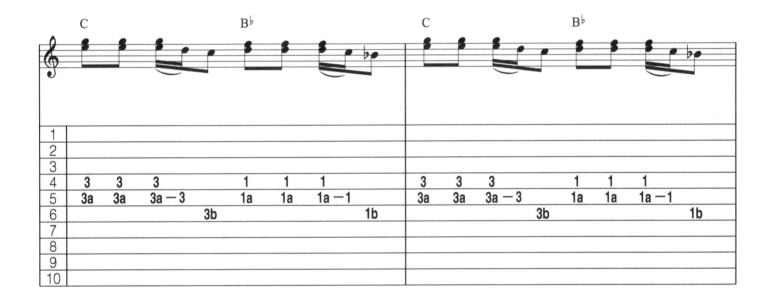

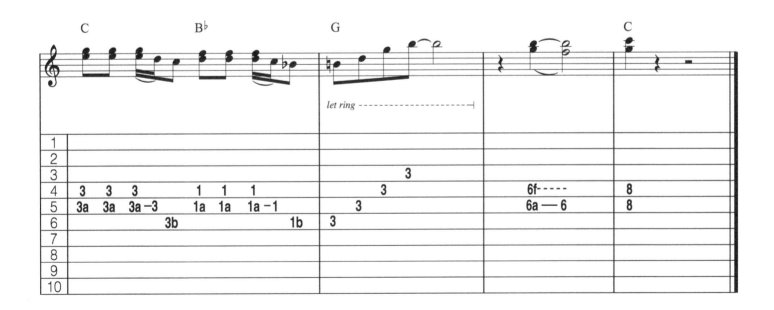

APPENDIX: MUSIC NOTATION

While tablature is great for showing us where to place the bar and which string to pick on the pedal steel, it does not tell us when to play the notes in the music: there's pitch, but no rhythm. For this we should learn to read some standard notation. Learning to read the same music that other musicians use also helps us communicate with them better. Here are some basics on music reading.

THE STAFF

Music is written in **notes** on a **staff**. The staff has five lines with four spaces between them. Where a note is written on the staff determines its pitch (highness or lowness). At the beginning of the staff is a **clef sign**. Most melodies are written in the treble clef.

Each line and space of the staff has a letter name. The lines are (from bottom to top) **E–G–B–D–F**, which you can remember as **E**very **G**ood **B**oy **D**oes **F**ine. The spaces are (from bottom to top) **F–A–C–E**, which spells "**Face**."

The lines and spaces together spell the musical alphabet using the first seven letters of the English alphabet, A through G. Once G is reached, the musical alphabet starts over. Two different notes with the same letter name, for instance E on the first line and E on the fourth space, are said to be an **octave** (eight notes) apart.

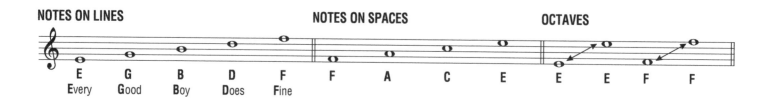

The staff is divided into several parts by **bar lines**. The space between two bar lines is called a **measure** (also known as a "**bar**"). To end a piece of music a **double bar line** is placed on the staff.

Each measure contains a group of **beats**. Beats are the steady pulse of music. You respond to the pulse or beat when you tap your foot.

TIME SIGNATURE

The top number tells you how many beats are in one measure.
The bottom number tells you what kind of note will receive one beat.

NOTES

Notes indicate the length (number of counts) of musical sound.

You can tell which pitch to play by the position of a note on the staff, and how long to play it by its shape.

RESTS

In addition to notes, songs may also contain silences, or **rests**—beats in which you play or sing nothing at all. A rest is a musical pause. Rests are like notes in that they have their own rhythmic values, instructing you how long (or for how many beats) to pause:

EIGHTH NOTES

If you divide a quarter note in half, you get an **eighth note**. An eighth note looks like a quarter note, but with a flag on its stem.

EIGHTH NOTES

Two eighth notes equal one quarter note. To help you keep track of the beat, consecutive eighth notes are connected with a **beam** instead of having flags.

To count eighth notes, divide the beat into two, and use "and" between the beats. Practice this first by counting aloud while tapping your foot on the beat, and then by clapping the notes while counting and foot-tapping.

Eighth rests are counted the same way, but you pause instead of playing.

TIES AND DOTS

The **tie** is a curved line that connects two notes of the same pitch. When you see a tie, play the first note and then hold it for the total value of both notes. Try this example with your open fifth (B) string.

Ties are useful when you need to extend the value of a note across the bar line.

Another useful way to extend the value of a note is to use a **dot**. A dot extends any note by one-half its value. Most common is the **dotted half note**, which extends a half note so that it lasts for three beats. If a measure starts with a dotted half note, then any note written right after if would start on beat 4.

INTERVALS

The smallest distance, or **interval**, between two notes is called a **half step**. If you play any note on your guitar and then play another note one fret higher or lower, you have just played a half step. If you move two frets higher (two half steps up) or two frets lower (two half steps down), you have moved one **whole step**. For us steel players, pedals and levers are also used to lower or raise certain notes by half or whole steps.

ACCIDENTALS

Any note can be raised or lowered by a half step by placing an **accidental** directly before it.

SHARP (♯) ⟶ Raises a note one half step (one fret)
FLAT (♭) ⟶ Lowers a note one half step (one fret)
NATURAL (♮) ⟶ Cancels previously used sharp or flat

LEDGER LINES

Notes higher or lower than the range of the staff are written using ledger lines.

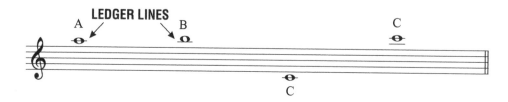

8va

If the notes are so high that ledger lines are hard to read, then the music can be written "*al ottava*," which is Italian for "at the octave," indicated by the symbol **8va** above the staff. The music is then played an octave higher than written.